FULL

HOW TO QUIT LIVING WITH THE GLASS HALF EMPTY

TABLE OF CONTENTS

To my love Kaleb, I could not have done this without your wholehearted support and sacrifice

A WORD FROM THE AUTHOR

"Come with me by yourselves to a quiet place and get some rest," (Mark 6:31, NIV).

In the quiet place with God, we are restored. Our minds are bathed in light and our vision is sharpened. In the quiet place with God, we are prepared for what lies ahead. Here, the impossible is possible, the broken is restored, and hopelessness is illuminated by heavenly possibilities.

My hope for your time with this book is that you will learn the process of washing your thoughts in the water of Christ's fullness, so your life will overflow with abundance.

Mornings in His quiet, reassuring presence made this writing possible. This devotional is a simple look into what the Holy Spirit has gently woven into my soul over the past four years—a look into what's being said in the quiet. I hope this spurs you on, and I hope it creates a deeper yearning for more of God.

Thank you for picking up this devotional. Thank you for giving me the honor of your time. May this book be a helpful ally on your literary quest for encountering more of God.

As you go through this devotional, I beg you to shut the door to your room and get alone with God daily. Listen to Him. Read the Bible; test everything you hear with His word. I promise I will probably get things wrong. I am not perfect; we are all simply seeking the only One who is. I may say something you disagree with, but I will give you countless opportunities to understand why God is the only One we should ever put our full confidence in.

Here's to joyful, soul-sharpening reading my friend!

So much love,

Alexis Klein

INTRODUCTION

So, what does "full" mean? In the book of John, Jesus reminds us that the enemy doesn't want us to experience the fullness God has for us. "The thief comes only in order to steal, kill and destroy. I have come that they may have and enjoy life and have it in abundance [to the full, till it overflows]" (John 10:10, AMP).

So, the Devil gets sneaky; he plays dirty, he does whatever he can to keep us living with our glasses half empty. But, Jesus came to fill our cups, our lives to overflow.

As we venture on, I must remind myself and you that once we have received Christ and are baptized by His Holy Spirit, then fullness is in us. But, we must walk in this fullness! We must "put on" those attributes of Christ that will usher us into living full, not just being full.

We must identify ourselves with Christ's death on the cross and step into the power of His resurrection. So, what does this resurrection power means for us?

>We are new creations
>We are heirs to the kingdom
>We are anointed, holy, called
>We are loved without condition
>We have power over darkness

But too many of us are not living like it. We live defeated lives, trapped by our own feelings or circumstances. We waste so much time looking for a win when the one who already won is alive in us!

Today we will step into all God has for us by finally plugging up those holes we've been drilling in the bottom of our cups. We're shutting up the lies and the false beliefs that have caused the fullness of God to drain right out of us —leaving us half empty.

The great paradox of fullness in Christ is that we must totally empty ourselves if we are to be totally full of Him. May these broken pieces of my story be an encouragement to you and how you too can pursue a life that's full, in a world that can be so incredibly draining.

Day 1 of this devotional brings you to my own day one of understanding and apprehending fullness. Each day after, you'll get a firsthand look into my own life experiences and how I learned the ebb and flow of living a full life that's overflowing.

"In Christ, you have been brought to fullness. He is the head over every power and authority."

Colossians 2:10, NIV

DAY 1: WHEN I REALIZED WHY MY CUP WAS CONSTANTLY DRAINING

ALL OF US WANT TO MAKE AN IMPACT IN THE WORLD; BUT TO LEAVE A MARK THAT MATTERS, WE MUST LOCK ONTO THE BELIEF THAT WE LACK NOTHING.

I hopped on the bus, hurriedly sat on the nearest seat and sunk into my thoughts. As the oak trees blurred past, a new truth came into focus.

With a swipe of my index finger, God met me on social media. The post I saw read, "I am completely satisfied in Christ. I lack nothing because I am hidden in His fullness. I live my life in the overflow of Jesus Christ."

That fleeting glance stirred something, something that would forever alter my walk with God.

The bus's screeching brakes startled my internal dialogue. As I walked down sorority row, giant houses and chatty college students flooded my view. When I finally made it to my sorority house—a 23-bedroom mansion that housed 50 girls—I sat down to write a paper. As you can imagine, it wasn't quiet.

Thankfully, my incessant internal chatter often doubles as noise-cancelling headphones…except for today. No matter how many thoughts inundated my mind, I couldn't block out the girl next to me. "Y'all, my hand really hurts still," she complained.

My next wave of thoughts stunned me: "You lack nothing, so you can pray for her to be healed." I typed louder to drown out that notion. I didn't want to pray. I didn't know what to say. I didn't know how she would take it. People were around. "It's too weird," I decided. "I'm not doing it."

It seemed the louder I typed, the more she complained about her hand. The more she complained, the more I felt it—that sensation in my bones—the Holy Spirit nudging me to obey, daring me to trust: **I lack nothing.**

Inhale. "Look up from your screen," I told myself.

"So I know this is super weird but I've seen God heal people before. Could I pray for you? I think he can heal your hand!" I blurted out.

Like a bug on a windshield—splat. Much to my relief, my splattering word vomit released all my internal pressure and ended all of my arguments.

"Really?" she said. "Yeah why not... you can pray for my hand."

"God please heal every fiber of this hand and restore it to perfection in Jesus name, amen," I exhaled. Nothing happened, except a somewhat awkward silence. I finished my paper and left.

The next day, she walked into the house. I sat typing at a desk and she made small talk with other girls in the room. Turning, she saw me and shouted, "Alexis, what did you do?! I woke up this morning and my hand was completely better!"

———

In the most perfect, unassuming of ways, **God showed up.** He showed up to heal, and He showed up to remind me that His children are full and we lack absolutely nothing.

I don't share this story to say that unless we see someone get healed we aren't full. I've prayed for many people to get healed—my husband included —and haven't seen it happen yet. But that certainly doesn't diminish the fullness of God's power and presence at work in us. It's the belief that I lack nothing that even gave me the courage to pursue what Jesus instructs us in Matthew 10:8, "heal the sick..."

I share this story because I want to remind myself and you that God marked us with the purpose of carrying His life-changing presence in this world, and He made us good enough, full enough to do it.

Fill Your Cup

What are some desires you've felt stirring on your heart lately? What pursuits
have you put off because this voice keeps telling you that you just don't
have enough (enough smarts, courage, holiness, money) to start? Write it
out and commit to doing just one of those things this week!
Remember, **you lack nothing.**

_____

_____

_____

_____

_____

_____

_____

_____

_____

"So we fix our eyes not on what is seen, but on what is unseen, since what is seen is temporary, but what is unseen is eternal."

2 Corinthians 4:18, NIV

DAY 2: WHEN FEAR OF A BORING LIFE DRAINED MY CUP

EVEN IN THE MUNDANE MOMENTS, THERE IS A DEEP, SATISFYING FULLNESS AVAILABLE TO US, IF WE WOULD LOOK BEYOND WHAT WE CAN SEE AND PEER DEEPER INTO THE HEART OF GOD.

A few years back, my mom and I hosted a guest speaker named Kim at our house. Kim was getting ready to share her incredible life story. While we all snacked and chatted around our kitchen island waiting for the story to start, I overheard a woman talking with my mom. "My life has just been so boring. Nothing interesting has really happened," she said.

A rock formed in my stomach. "A boring life?" I thought. "I can't bear the idea. What if when I'm middle-aged, I'm sitting around talking about how unexciting my life has been? How boring?!"

Anxiety and panic spilled over my soul. But then I remembered, "I am full. I will lack no good thing (even when I'm older, even if my kids rule my schedule, even if laundry and cooking consume my everyday) because I am hidden in the overflow of Jesus."

Phew, meltdown averted.

—

I realized something in that moment. If we're really doing this Christian thing right, life with God can't be boring. It is impossible to spend each day with the Creator of the Universe and be bored. If I am bored, God is not the problem—I am. If you are bored, it's time to assess if you're really living the full life He has for you or if you are settling for a life that's half empty.

God wants us to become people so immersed in His presence that heavenly happenings seep out from our souls even in the mundane. There is purpose and fullness to be found whether you are single or a homemaker or a single mom. Our station in life doesn't reflect the unchanging truth of our identity in Christ, it adds to it. It creates another nuance of how He's moving and what He's doing in our lives in the specific season we are in.

But, getting on God's wavelength and finding deep meaning in the ordinary takes practice. Over the years, I've had to get creative about finding purpose in my menial tasks like cooking and folding clothes. Sometimes when I'm at the stove, I will ask God who He wants us to invite to dinner this month. When I'm annoyed by how hectic my work schedule is, I ask God if there is anyone at my office He wants to reach. Or, I turn the task into an opportunity for gratitude.

There are so many opportunities to connect with Christ and His heart for us in the ordinary. So no matter where you are on your journey, just know that there is deeply satisfying intimacy available to us at every moment and boredom is not something we need to wallow in!

Fill Your Cup

If you've found yourself bored or apathetic toward God, maybe you've slipped into lukewarm living. I've been there. So take this time to fire up the flame again. Ask the Holy Spirit to open up your eyes to the grandeur and goodness of God, so you can start living a life that's full and overflowing. Write down what you hear the Lord speaking as you lay yourself before Him.

_____

_____

_____

_____

_____

_____

_____

_____

_____

"Brothers and sisters, if someone is caught in a sin, you who live by the Spirit should restore that person gently. But watch yourselves, or you also may be tempted."

Galatians 6:1, NIV

DAY 3: WHEN THE SHAME OF SEXUAL SIN DRAINED MY CUP

CASUAL SIN COSTS US THE EXPERIENCE OF GOD'S EXTRAVAGANT PLEASURE IN US.

One night when my husband and I were still dating, we opted for a movie night.

Now it's important to set the scene: we were each other's first experience in a Christian relationship, and we both marveled daily at the goodness of God, which He revealed to us through our dating. In fact, through this man, the Holy Spirit healed me of emotional hurts I'd carried for years. Without a doubt, this relationship was heaven-sent for God's glory and for our good.

But, he and I both had a past of struggling with sexual sin—prior to us knowing each other and God.

So, that night we were on his couch. My head rested on his shoulder and my feet stretched out to share his foot rest. At some point he reclined his chair back and I proceeded to scoot closer so I could recline with him.

Immediately, I felt a pinch in my spirit. Holy Spirit made it clear that it was for my good not to recline with him. Yet, in this second-long interaction with the Holy Spirit, I declared the conviction petty, so I ignored it. That exact exchange happened more times than I'd like to admit.

Nearly every time I crossed that physical line in my spirit, I spoiled the night for myself. The drive home phone calls always sounded something like this "Ugh, I just think we shouldn't have done that. I feel so bad. I feel so guilty. I'm sorry, let's try better next time."

I was so frustrated with myself and with my weakness and disobedience that I often spent the night just ranting about how we "should've tried harder to do better."

Eventually, the shame of my disobedience piled on so high that the fullness and happiness I once felt was gone. Sin will do that to you.

My disobedience quenched the Holy Spirit and made it impossible to enjoy the heaven-sent blessing of that relationship. God put in place good, healthy, loving boundaries—boundaries that helped me enjoy His blessings —and I trampled upon them. I walked outside of the protection of my Father and the consequences were miserable.

But, God.

After months of rattling my emotions, carrying around guilt and condemning myself, I decided to confess my sins. I mustered up the courage to tell my mentor about disobeying some of the boundaries God had placed.

She received me with grace and kindness. That's what our job is here on earth, to restore each other gently—because God uses that to plug up those holes of shame and to fill our cups to overflow once more.

Fill Your Cup

Is there any unconfessed sin in your life that's causing you to feel half empty all the time, weighed down by shame and guilt? Get it all out on these lines and ask the Holy Spirit to restore you gently and give you strength to keep walking in His power.

If you have a trusted friend or mentor, give them a call and let God use them to love you back together with kindness and grace.

_____

_____

_____

_____

_____

_____

"But God demonstrates his own
love for us in this:

While we were still sinners, Christ
died for us."

Romans 5:8, NIV

DAY 4: WHEN BEING PASSIVE-AGGRESSIVE DRAINED MY CUP

LIVING WITH SOMEONE REVEALS AN ENTIRELY DIFFERENT SIDE OF THEM, A SIDE WE MAY NOT LIKE; YET, CHRIST KNOCKS AT THE DOOR OF OUR HEARTS, WANTING TO LIVE AMONG EVEN THE UNLOVELY PARTS OF US.

"Okay, who keeps leaving these dirty dishes in the sink?" my roommate stammered.

"I'm not sure," I replied. "Maybe we can leave a note. Or maybe we just let the dishes keep piling up so they get the hint."

Staring at the sink, we passive-aggressively decided to let the dishes pile up. As the stack grew higher, so did my irritability. With each day, I got more annoyed with the two roommates who might have been the culprits. The longer I refused to confront the problem directly, the harder it was to enjoy our friendship and revel in the fun of living together.

———

Whether it's a spouse, a friend, or a roommate, when you live with someone, you get a front-row seat to their flaws—and they get a front-row seat to yours. With each new quirk we discover, we may find ourselves liking the other person less and less. We may even find ourselves projecting onto Christ our own tendency to reject people when they frustrate us or don't meet our expectations.

But, Jesus knows every undesirable trait we posses, and He still desires closeness with us. He knows our every failure, sin, and flaw (past and present) yet His Holy Spirit desires to make His home in us. All we have to do? Ask the Holy Spirit to help us turn away from our sins, commit to living life God's way, and receive His unreasonably kind offer to move into our hearts.

Fill Your Cup

Before we come to know Christ, we're tempted to believe Jesus only wants the squeaky clean version of ourselves. We think He wants a roommate as perfect as He is—no dirty dishes, no dirty secrets. But how can we let Him cleanse us if we won't even let Him in the door?

Right now, take this moment to let Him in. Repent for any sin lurking in your heart. Inhale the acceptance of your heavenly Savior. Exhale all of the reasons you're just not good enough or clean enough for Him to live in you. Then, write Romans 5:8 until you sense yourself really grasping that truth: "But God demonstrates His own love for us in this: While we were still sinners, Christ died for us." Remember, the love of Christ isn't something we could ever earn, it pre-dates our best efforts and our holiest prayers. So receive His gift of love knowing that He gives it just because He wants to.

_____

_____

_____

_____

_____

_____

_____

_____

_____

_____

"Do nothing out of selfish ambition or vain conceit. Rather, in humility value others above yourselves."

Philippians 2:3, NIV

DAY 5: WHEN SELF-FOCUS DRAINED MY CUP

SOMETIMES THE CURE TO FEELING EMPTY IS TO START FILLING OTHER PEOPLE'S CUPS.

Augusts in Louisiana are brutal. Not only does it reach up to 100 degrees, but the humidity is almost suffocating. Now imagine a day like that, and imagine you're wearing high heels, a tight-fitted dress, and makeup. Next? Add 200 girls to this scenario, jammed into a house, and forced to have hours of small talk.

This is sorority recruitment.

As a college sophomore, I was already in my sorority, which meant this year it was my responsibility to interview or "rush" girls. I was so nervous. What on earth could I possibly say to a complete stranger for TEN MINUTES? And not just one stranger, but dozens of strangers, party after party! It seems down right impossible—especially for an introvert like myself.

The first round of parties was a little rough. I was internally going through my own identity transformation with being a new Christian and I was still feeling a little bit uncertain of myself and finding Christian friends. I was wondering if it's even worth it to be doing this whole sorority thing.

But then it clicked: I am not the one with the short end of the stick here, they are. These poor girls are coming into a whole new school, trying to pave a whole new life for themselves, while figuring out who they are AND who they want to spend the next four years of college with—they are freaking out.

In a change of perspective, I made this day all about them and not at all about me. I had a blast from that moment forward. I was genuinely interested in knowing who they were, where they came from, what they were excited and nervous about.

Sometimes we feel empty simply because we're self-centered. We can get so consumed with how we're feeling or what our next move is and we can't even see the people right in front of us who need our genuine friendship and attention.

Making that shift in the dynamic caused those humid August afternoons to be some of my favorite memories in college. I loved the privilege of getting to be a kind and welcoming face to those new freshman. I loved learning how just a few sincere questions and a smile could melt the pressure and nervousness right off their shoulders.

———

That is who Jesus is to us. He is the friendly, kind presence who takes the pressures of life off our shoulders. That is who we are called to be. When we're emotionally and spiritually healthy, we have so much power. We can lean into conversations armed with encouragement, with eyes laser focused on the person behind the makeup and the jitters. We can walk into any room and strike any conversation to fill up someone else's cup and help them to step into the fullness God has for them.

Fill Your Cup

Take a minute to switch your thoughts from self-focused to others-focused. Who comes to mind as you think of someone whose cup you could fill this week? Maybe you can send them an encouraging text or a hand-written note or maybe even spend some quality time with them. Write down a person or two and then write out how you will fill their cup. Be extra intentional by choosing an exact date when you plan to do it. Get excited because you're going to love this!

_____

_____

_____

_____

_____

_____

_____

"It is for freedom that Christ has set us free..."

Galatians 5:1, NIV

DAY 6: WHEN WORRYING WHAT PEOPLE THOUGHT ABOUT ME DRAINED MY CUP

WHEN WE SIDE WITH PRIDE, OUR RELATIONSHIPS SUFFER. WHEN WE FREELY EXTEND LOVE, OUR RELATIONSHIPS ARE FULL.

As a brand new Christian, I church-hopped like it was a summer side hustle. I would sometimes go to multiple services at different churches in the same day. I was hungry for God.

One day, I invited a group of friends to church. The church I invited them to was very charismatic, as they call it. It wasn't your traditional service. So as my friends got up to leave, the surge of questions rushed.

"Do they think I'm crazy? Do they think God's crazy? Are they ever going to talk to me again?"

Right then and there, a shield rose up from within me and I felt the Holy Spirit urge me to drop it.

In that moment, I had the choice: choose my own pride and wind up harming my friendship because I was so insistent that they were judging me; or, drop my pride and choose to love them even if they thought I was weird. I decided: if people think I'm weird and don't want to be my friend, I will be okay. But I'm not going to carry around a worry that could threaten a non-threatened relationship.

———

Have you ever caught yourself creating an entire storyline of judgements and lies that people must be spreading about you? We can waste so much energy consumed with made-up accusations. All of that self-focused energy does nothing but distract us from inviting that friend to church, sharing the Gospel with that coworker, or flashing a smile at that neighbor.

To this day, I look back on that moment in church as a reference point for how I want to react in a time of feeling self-conscious and judged. The freedom I experienced to continue to love my two friends with sincerity and without an awkward aftertaste in my mouth showed me a whole new way of living.

This is how God wants us to live—free, unfettered by offense and regret.

Fill Your Cup

Is there a moment when you feared someone was judging you? Is there that one critical voice who rises up when you think about trying something new? Or is there a distinct memory you can point to where fear of judgement injured your relationship? Breathe deeply and then exhale as your Father's loving-kindness washes over you and that memory. Let Him help you extend the same forgiveness and freedom He extends to you.

Use these lines to write out this truth over your past, your present and your future: "I am full and I lack no good thing; I live in the overflow of Jesus Christ. I freely extend forgiveness to all those who have hurt me and I free them from my mind's memory reel of pain."

_____

_____

_____

_____

_____

_____

_____

_____

"And to know this love that surpasses knowledge—that you may be filled to the measure of all the fullness of God. Now to him who is able to do immeasurably more than all we ask or imagine, according to his power that is at work within us..."

Ephesians 3:19-20, NIV

DAY 7: WHEN FEARING SOMETHING BAD WOULD HAPPEN DRAINED MY CUP

WHEN JESUS SPENT 40 DAYS IN THE DESERT, FACING TEMPTATION OF EVERY KIND, HIS WEAPON OF CHOICE WAS THE WORD OF GOD. GRAB YOUR WEAPON AND FILL YOUR CUP.

During a week in college when none of my roommates were home, fear crept up my spine with each creak in our old house. "I'm going to get kidnapped," I thought, over and over again. Each night alone, I felt like the enemy was whispering death over me.

Then finally, after two nights of getting almost no sleep, I swiped my phone to call a friend. But as I went to call her, I thought, "Why am I bending to fear?"

I grabbed the book on my desk and flipped to Ephesians 3:17-21: "I pray that you, being rooted and established in love, may have power, together with all the Lord's holy people, to grasp how wide and long and high and deep is the love of Christ…"

As I spoke each line aloud, fear sulked into a corner. Finally I said, "Holy Spirit, please show me the depth of Jesus' love. I want to know it by experience. Do immeasurably more by taking this fear away from me."

Minutes later, I fell asleep.

As I slept, I had an incredibly vivid dream. There was a large concrete truck. You know, the big machines with large, slowly spinning containers.

Suddenly, the machine started churning a mixture. This mixture contained TV shows I had seen, song lyrics I had heard, movie clips I had watched. After all of these mixed together into a single blend of concrete, the truck slowly poured the liquid out to form a foundation. Once the concrete settled, cracks burst through the slab.

I understood the foundation to be my mind. I knew the Holy Spirit was showing me that everything I give attention to (social media, entertainment, music, etc.) affects my mind and spirit. The details of this vision were so specific that He even showed me exact moments in my childhood where fear took root.

I knew I needed help and that Jesus was the only One who could eradicate this old foundation. I knew He had the good kind of concrete, the kind that would harden into a fresh, solid slab of pure thought patterns and unspeakable peace.

Then, a jackhammer appeared in my dream. Reverberating on top of the cracked foundation, pieces went flying, until there was nothing left of that slab.

Over to my right I saw another concrete truck. In it, a pure mixture of wholeness and peace. The liquid concoction slowly poured out and settled as a perfectly pure, unblemished foundation. I understood that the key to a solid mental and spiritual foundation was to keep my eyes fixed on Christ and His word, His promises for my life.

———

Have you ever found yourself living in the land of your worst nightmares? Have you ever caught your thoughts traveling to places you don't even enjoy or want to be? When that happens, we have access to the most powerful weapon the world has ever seen—scripture.

We don't need to shove the fear away and just wait for it to resurface again, we need to introduce our biggest fears to God's bigger promises.

So, what do you fear? No matter what it is, know fear is not from God. The only way we will see positive changes in our thoughts, attitudes and behaviors is if we submit our fears to God and let Him do His perfect work in us.

Fill Your Cup

First John 4:18 says, "There is no fear in love, but perfect love casts out fear, because fear has to do with punishment. The one who fears is not made perfect in love."

Confront your fears right here and now. Write out what you're most afraid of and then write out scriptures that overcome that fear. If you need help, just do a quick search online for verses relating to fear or relating to a specific area where you're struggling. Meditate on scripture until you physically experience the threat and fear dwindle.

If there are areas of your life where fear drains your cup, then God has not been given control over that area. Give Him control in this moment. Holy Spirit make these truths real to us as we live out today.

_____

_____

_____

_____

_____

_____

_____

_____

_____

"Whether you turn to the right or to the left, your ears will hear a voice behind you, saying, 'This is the way; walk in it.'"

Isaiah 30:21, NIV

DAY 8: WHEN FEAR OF MAKING THE WRONG DECISION DRAINED MY CUP

INDECISION WILL DRAIN YOUR CUP AND PARALYZE YOUR LIFE; BUT FULL TRUST IN CHRIST WILL PROPEL YOU TO PLACES YOU NEVER DREAMED.

Pacing back and forth, each creaking floorboard reinforcing the weight of my impending decision, I had a few days left to give my answer.

Should I go to that Bible college or should I take that public relations internship? What if I make the wrong move? What if I mess up God's plan for my life? What if I end up miserable and bored?

The anxiety of my senior year of college was absolutely crippling. Each day, I teetered on a see-saw of indecision and fear.

"Lord if you just tell me what to do, I will do it. Just give me a hint. I'm willing, I'm ready. What is it already?"

———

Ever been there? Ever felt like your next move could be THE move that would forever alter your life? From high school to college to marriage, I've carried that crippling anxiety of "what if I make the wrong choice?"

And it's served my life in no way other than to create wrinkles, zits, and annoyingly long phone calls with everyone except THE ONE who held my peace.

If you have ever experienced what I'm talking about, you know how much it just sucks. But here's what more than a decade of decision-making has taught me:

> 1. No one wants God's will for my life more than God Himself. So if I haven't heard anything more specific about my next decision, then I have to eventually trust that He's given me all of the info I need to take the next step.

2. God doesn't always give me the play-by-play *before* asking me to step out in faith. If I know everything ahead of time, I'll never have the chance to "walk by faith and not by sight" (2 Cor. 5:7).

3. God is ALWAYS, ALWAYS, ALWAYS, after something deeper than just our physical choices.

Although it may be answers we're specifically after, know that God is after our heart. More than anything, He wants us to walk in the security of His love for us, so we can make decisions in boldness, expectancy and peace.

Let go of the notion that "if I make the wrong call, God is going to hate me." Step into your next big decision with the perspective that "God will tell me just what I need to know, God has filled me with Himself, and with Him by my side I can make decisions in peace and safety."

While waiting on Him for a direct answer, we must choose to focus fully on His all-sufficient presence. In bowing our hearts in worship, our grips loosen and our agendas fall casually to the side.

Fill Your Cup

Maybe today you find yourself at a fork in the road, stressing over what the next best move is. Or maybe you're at a dead end and you don't know how or when or where you could possibly move from the place you are in life. Or, perhaps you're all settled into your routine and your career and you should just be asking God, "What do you want me to do next, Lord?"

No matter where you are today, take time right now to write out the choices before you and then loosen your grip on the belief that it's all up to you.

Receive the irrevocable truth of fullness in Christ that comes regardless of which path you choose. Let God breathe a new perspective into your soul, so you will be steady no matter what life brings.

"They [the righteous] will be like a tree planted by the water that sends out its roots by the stream. It does not fear when heat comes; its leaves are always green. It has no worries in a year of drought and never fails to bear fruit."

Jeremiah 17:8, NIV

DAY 9: WHEN GRADUATION DAY DRAINED MY CUP

EVEN IN LIFE'S DESERT, GOD MAKES A WAY FOR US TO THRIVE.

Graduation morning. Three weeks after my dad suddenly passed away. Eyes sunken from lack of sleep, my mind awake from the collision of death and grief and scholarly celebration.

"Did I sleep through my ceremony?" I thought, as the sun spilled through the windows. "No, it's still early." I woke up before my alarm. "Lord, I don't want to do this," I prayed, as I shut my eyes tightly. "I can't do this."

"Who can I call? Can Nicole ride with me to our graduation? Am I okay to drive? What if I have a mental breakdown? Will my mom be okay today? What about my brother and grandma? What if they get in a car accident on the way here? I won't have anymore family at all."

These thoughts bombarded my half-conscious self.

"Jesus," I whispered. "Jesus," I whispered again. I learned this prayer just a week before my dad passed. I was sitting in my sorority house, incredibly stressed about my final project, when my roommate Leah walked in to check on me.

"I'm stressed!" I snapped. Then she looked at me with a calm, reassuring voice and said, "It's going to be okay. When I get really stressed, I inhale and exhale, breathing "Jesus, Jesus, Jesus" until I feel Him.

In this moment before graduation, I was so thankful for that moment and the gift of this spiritual discipline. While I was walking through life, toward a painful bend in the road, God was scattering seeds that I didn't even know I would need. He was following through on His declaration that the righteous would flourish even in life's droughts (Jer. 17:8).

On this particular day, flourishing wasn't stunning or exciting. It was a gut-wrenching yet simple act of putting my feet on the floor. It was showing up to an auditorium of thousands of excited graduates and their families. It was walking across that stage and lifting a smile just long enough for the picture.

If I could see that day from heaven's perspective, I am certain it was marvelous. It was yet another reason for unending praise to our Heavenly Father who deeply meets our needs and gently lifts our heads and our feet out of bed.

———

Maybe you've experienced a time in your life when victory and triumph was just the simple act of putting two feet on the floor. Maybe it was just taking that next breath or writing that last line.

Know this, not one of us will escape this beautiful, gut-wrenching, miraculous life without knowing the significance of just making it another day. There will come a time when everything in you will feel like it cannot possibly go on, but then you will remember to whisper the sweet name of Jesus.

"Jesus, Jesus, Jesus" was my song of worship, my song of lament, my desperate plea for help; and with each whisper, I felt Him steadily filling me up until I could put both feet on the ground.

Fill Your Cup

Are you experiencing your own personal drought, wondering how you're supposed to put your feet on the floor?

Meditate on Jeremiah 17:8 and the truth that God will help you flourish even in times of drought. Breathe deeply, whispering the name of your sweet, ever-present help in times of need.

Then, write what He's speaking to you.

_____

_____

_____

_____

_____

_____

_____

_____

"I say to myself, 'The LORD is my portion; therefore I will wait for him.'"

Lamentations 3:24, NIV

DAY 10: WHEN LONELINESS DRAINED MY CUP

SOMETIMES IT TAKES UTTER LONELINESS TO EXPERIENCE THE
OVERWHELMING REALITY OF CHRIST'S NEARNESS.

Rolling to the stop sign, I was struck by the sprawling colors in the sky. No
sooner did I breathe in the awe of God's creation did I think, "Who can I
enjoy this pretty evening with? I have no one. My friends don't live in town. I
don't have a boyfriend. Why hasn't my best friend called me in weeks?
Doesn't she know how badly I'm hurting? I told her I really need a friend."

Sorrow seeped in and awe of the fall weather seeped out.

"Lord, you are my portion," I whispered. Like a sword, those words whipped
through my thoughts. Tears welled and trickled down my cheeks, as I came
around the corner on my way home.

That year had been particularly hard with losing my father. Most of my
friends still lived in the city where I went to college, and I didn't have just
anyone to spend my time with.

In 2016, I had a lot of moments like that, where my mind would search for
plans or people to hang out with, and I would resort to spending the
afternoon with my mom, writing, or sometimes just being sad.

As much as I wanted things to be different, I couldn't change my situation. I
couldn't change that my friends lived out of town. I couldn't force my friends
to call me. The Lord was my only option.

It sounds depressing, but that season was working something into me that I
don't think existed before—experiential knowledge that Jesus really is
sufficient for me; He really does make me full, lacking nothing.

The AMP version of Lamentations 3:24 reads "The Lord is my
portion and my inheritance," says my soul; "Therefore I have hope in
Him and wait expectantly for Him."

This verse is a call to remember two realities: the Lord is totally sufficient for me in my pain and loss, but He is also working on something that is cause for hope and expectancy in my life.

It's not that He desired for my life to be spent in isolation like that forever. He was walking with me from one season to the next, and there was cause for me to be hopeful and expectant in what He was going to do.

———

Have you ever felt like you were in an abyss of anxiety because you desperately wanted human connection but there was just no one to call? Like the people you've reached out to are too busy to care? Have you ever been so lonely you cried? Felt so isolated and misunderstood?

It's okay, me too.

But if we'll let Him in, Jesus will show us His all-sufficiency. He will meet us right in the midst of our own suffering and He'll fill our emptiness with the fullness of Himself.

That afternoon in the car, I don't think I could have had the strength on my own to declare "You are my portion, Lord." I believe the Helper, the Holy Spirit came up under me and gave those words to me. What a gift that the God of the entire Universe would take the time to lift my heavy heart while I was at a stop sign. I'm no one noteworthy in the eyes of the world, but I am someone deeply and fully loved in the eyes of Jesus. So are you.

Fill Your Cup

Take a few minutes to meditate on Lamentations 3:24. Write out the things in your world right now that may be weighing you down—the thoughts that may be causing you sorrow and the pains you're still working through. Then, write "The Lord is my portion" as many times as it takes for you to start to experience the weight and gift of that truth. What once felt empty will begin to feel whole and full again.

"Praise be to the God and Father of our Lord Jesus Christ, the Father of compassion and the God of all comfort, who comforts us in all our troubles, so that we can comfort those in any trouble with the comfort we ourselves receive from God. For just as we share abundantly in the sufferings of Christ, so also our comfort abounds through Christ."

2 Corinthians 1:3-5, NIV

DAY 11: WHEN SELF-PITY DRAINED MY CUP

THERE IS A TIME TO HEAL FROM TRAUMA AND THERE IS A TIME TO HELP OTHERS DO THE SAME. WE MUST DISCERN WHAT TIME IT IS FOR US.

"Alexis, it's time to stop with the pity party and start loving on people around you. The world desperately needs me." I was sitting in my room one evening, writing in my journal, and I heard those words in my spirit. Sounds harsh to tell a girl who had recently lost her dad. But I knew it was coming. Not only did I know it was coming, but I knew that I had no more excuses.

For a few months, the Holy Spirit had been dealing with me about wallowing. I was using my grief as an excuse to not engage with things I knew God was calling me to do.

When I would feel Him tugging at my heart to share the Gospel with someone or spend time with someone, I would tell Him, "I'm not really ready for that, God. I just lost my dad and can't really handle other people's needs right now."

But I knew God was moving me into a new season.

It took me a bit to realize that His means of helping me heal required me to pour myself out, so He could pour Himself in, so I could pour His spirit onto those around me.

The day after that revelation, I pulled into my driveway and noticed the painter, Mr. H was at our house. Days earlier, I learned that Mr. H had just lost his grand-daughter in a tragic murder.

I felt that unction of the Holy Spirit nudging me to share something with Mr. H. But I resisted. It was a song, just a few lines of scripture I had sung into the voice notes on my phone while driving home. Even though it wasn't very melodic, I knew I had to do it.

So, awkwardly, I walked up the stairs to where he was. My heart beat rapidly, while compassion flooded my veins. "Mr. H," I said. "I'm so sorry about your grand-daughter."

"Thank you," he replied solemnly.

"I know this is odd, but I feel like the Lord wants me to share this song with you. I'm going to send it to your phone."

"Oh, okay" he said in a quiet, heartbroken voice.

I left.

The next day, I saw Mr. H again. His eyes welling with tears, he looked at me and said, "I have been asking God to give me an answer, and He finally gave it to me through your song."

The tears were mutual and the fullness of God welled up in me and flowed out.

What a kind Father we have.

———

Are you stuck somewhere? On something? Or someone? Is there a broken record that needs to be fixed? Have you ever found yourself hung up on something that happened to you—or to someone you love—and you just kept rewinding the tape? Have you ever spent weeks, months or even years dissecting exactly what was said, exactly how it happened, only to realize that no matter how many times you look at that event, you're still not healed or over it?

We all have or will experience that reality at some point, and God is gentle and patient to see us through our hurts and our losses. But He doesn't want us to stay there. He wants us to channel the comfort He's shown us so that we can comfort those around us who are hurting.

Fill Your Cup

Take time in this moment to do a mental health check and see if there is any memory you keep replaying in the background. See if there are unresolved feelings that keep bubbling up from the surface.

Then, write them out. Ask the Holy Spirit to give you His perspective, to strengthen you to move forward in wholeness and healing so you can live out 2 Corinthians 1:3-5 and comfort others with Christ's comfort you've received.

_____

_____

_____

_____

_____

_____

_____

_____

"Behold, You have made my days as handbreadths, And my lifetime as nothing in Your sight; Surely every man at his best is a mere breath. Selah."

Psalm 39:5, NASB

DAY 12: WHEN GRIEF DRAINED MY CUP

WHEN THE PAINS OF LIFE DRILL HOLES IN OUR GLASSES, THE FLOOD OF GRATITUDE FILLS US BACK UP AGAIN.

Springtime in New Orleans is the most exhilarating time in the world. The aroma of sweet honeysuckle flowers flood the sidewalks, the buzz of first-time visitors and returning travelers fills the streets, and the reminder of renewal permeates the hearts of the locals.

Not to mention, springtime is the best time for festivals. From the bayou to the French Quarter, there is always a way to connect with your community and culture.

So last spring, my husband Kaleb, my sister-in-law, brother-in-law and I decided to ride our bikes down to the French Quarter. The four of us live super close to the Quarter and the fresh air beckoned us to enjoy the French Quarter Fest—not to mention, it's a free festival, so these penny-pinchers were there.

My dad loved the French Quarter. Most weekends you could find him in the Don Juan's Cigar Shop smoking a cigar and watching the passerbys on Decatur Street. As kids, my brother and I grew up getting dragged down to the French Quarter for fresh muffulettas and beignets.

Ever since my dad died, going to the Quarter feels different. But today, it was just glorious. We ate beignets, we sat in Jackson Square listening to music, and we caught up on our lives.

A few hours later, we said our goodbyes and biked back home. Kaleb and I were in the kitchen getting ready to cook dinner. We turned on some jazz music, danced, laughed—that's when it hit me, in the middle of a laugh.

Dad. Thoughts of him flashed through my mind. Grief does not warn you when it's coming.

In the middle of a moment, with my husband of five months, in the throws of marital bliss, my overflowing cup quickly seeped into pain.

My poor husband—so caught off guard by my sudden swing in temperament asked, "What's wrong, Alexis?"

"I just really miss my dad," I sobbed.

———

It was in the middle of a moment, a conversation between my dad and my mom, when my dad suddenly took his last breath and came face to face with the love of His life, Jesus.

Life is so fleeting. We are so fragile. For this reason, we must give ourselves grace to breathe. We must give ourselves space to Selah. Selah is the word the Psalmist David often used at the end of his prayers of ascension to instruct the reader to pause and think calmly of that which is good.

May we learn the balance between welcoming the sorrow and remembering the blessing. May we hold life and its brevity, family and its bond, even loss and its heaviness within the gentle confines of Christ's redemptive promise.

Fill Your Cup

Have you ever had a moment of bliss hijacked by an unwelcome intruder like grief? Have you ever felt the joy of life seep right out of your glass and expose your fragility? It's times like these that make me realize how important it is to have a bank of gratitude stored up in your soul.

From our deep pit of grief, God will dig an even deeper well of gratitude, and when we let that spring up in us, everything else will seem to spring up too.

Write down five things you are grateful for today, remembering that life is fragile and our days are numbered, so we may as well fill our inner world with thankfulness.

"But you, O LORD, are a shield about me, my glory, and the lifter of my head."

Psalm 3:3, ESV

DAY 13: WHEN EARTHLY THOUGHTS DRAINED MY CUP

EARTHLY THOUGHTS DRAIN YOUR CUP, WHILE HEAVENLY THOUGHTS LIFT YOUR HEAD.

I broke up with Kaleb in college. I was terrified of marriage and his certainty about us scared me. The first night after we broke up, I wailed uncontrollably in my roommate's arms. She had to sleep next to me because I was nearly inconsolable.

Then, my friend Calah called. She said something that keeps coming back to me all these years later: "I'm praying that heavenly thoughts replace your earthly thoughts."

Today, as I drove home from work, I thought about what she had told me.

For whatever reason, I spent the entire day consumed with how much I hate death. This isn't unusual after losing my dad. I often think about how I hope I don't die young, how I hope Kaleb won't end up spending the rest of his life with someone else because I'm gone, or how I hope we get to grow old together.

At five o'clock, finally exhausted by my own thoughts, I whispered, "Holy Spirit, please give me heavenly thoughts instead of earthly ones."

Before the sentence was over, I heard God's calming, loving voice say, "Even when you die in this life, eventually you and Kaleb will both be in heaven and those days in Heaven will never end."

Forty minutes later, I finally stopped sobbing. Of course I know there is no marriage in heaven; I know I my earthly affections will be eclipsed by the presence of Jesus. But Jesus knew I didn't need to hear that. He knew His daughter just needed to be comforted in that moment with another truth.

The more I leaned into His words, the more my joy multiplied. "I will see my dad and my grandma, my great aunt and my grandpas," I thought. This perspective shift of an eternal day with nothing but family from every generation, nothing but joy unending, lifted my head and my spirit.

———

In Revelation 21:4 we read, "He will wipe away every tear from their eyes, and death shall be no more, neither shall there be mourning, nor crying, nor pain anymore, for the former things have passed away."

What a heavenly thought to lift the heaviness of loss. One day, all of the pain and hurt we experience will be nothing but a distant memory. It will be something that once held us but now has no power. May that promise of eternity lift whatever load you are carrying today.

Fill Your Cup

If you're carrying earthly thoughts of fear, angst or negativity, lift them up to your Father in heaven. Ask Him to do one of his divine exchanges: your earthly thoughts for His heavenly thoughts. Write out the new perspective He's offering you today as you meditate on the truth that He is the lifter of your head and He will wipe away every tear from your eyes.

_____
_____
_____
_____
_____

"Don't you see how wonderfully kind, tolerant, and patient God is with you? Does this mean nothing to you? Can't you see that his kindness is intended to turn you from your sin?"

Romans 2: 4, NLT

DAY 14: WHEN PETTY FIGHTS DRAINED MY CUP

WITH ACCESS TO THE WORLD'S DEEPEST WELL OF PATIENCE AND KINDNESS, WE CAN OVERCOME ANY ANNOYANCE OUR RELATIONSHIPS THROW AT US.

"Pastor Anthony," I said. "Let's talk about verses for the ceremony. I would really like 'Be completely humble and gentle, bearing with one another in love. Make every effort to keep unity of the spirit through the bond of peace' in Ephesians 4:2-3."

"Really?" he asked surprised. "When you are married," he continued "the two become one flesh. It doesn't get more unified that that."

"I guess I never thought about that," I said. "But it also talks about being humble and gentle and we really need that to keep peace in our home."

"That's true," he said. "But understand, you two are bonded together by God. Unity is always your reality."

I have to say, that first year of marriage didn't always feel so holy and unified. We had some *petty* arguments. Like the time I chopped bell peppers "too thickly" for Kaleb and he felt the need to let me know that. Or the time Kaleb sternly pleaded that I please ring out the sponge so it doesn't stay sopping wet. Or, here's the kicker, the time I told him I wouldn't even be sad if his 20-year-old bird died!

How unifying does that sound? But God's kindness and patience followed me in those early fights in our marriage. He brought me to understand that when Kaleb and I argue or disagree, we can do so from a mutual place of inner peace because we're working things out in the safety of our covenant promise to each other and to God. That's the beauty and joy of marriage, the permanent unity of our souls, contending for each other.

———

Have you ever found yourself convicted in the middle of an argument? I certainly felt it when I told Kaleb I wouldn't be sad if his bird died. It's not the greatest feeling. But, the very act of God convicting us should remind us just how kind He is. He loves us too much to let us keep making the same fatal mistakes in our relationships.

While it may seem like we can't be full unless our other half is completely on board, this isn't true. We are full solely on the basis of Jesus Christ. But if both people will come together and submit to the voice of the Holy Spirit, it is much easier to experience the joy of unity in marriage with the mutual understanding that we live from Christ's precious overflow of fullness.

May we encourage our spouses and ourselves in the truth that Jesus has given us a deep well that we can draw from whenever we want—a well full of grace for each other, peace for the day, and kindness for the moment.

Fill Your Cup

For those of us still on Earth today, the reality of God's kindness and patience is evident. We're still here, which means He's still granting us the privilege to turn from our sins and be reconciled to Him.

Is there a reoccurring sin that's draining your cup of fullness? Is there a petty fight or choice you're continually making that's sabotaging your most intimate relationships? Take this moment to write those out and then ask God to forgive you. Ask the Holy Spirit to strengthen your resolve to do better today so you can keep living a life that's filled to overflow.

_____

_____

_____

_____

"He is before all things, and in him all things hold together."

Colossians 1:17, NIV

DAY 15: WHEN MY OWN STRENGTH DRAINED MY CUP

OUR OWN DOWNFALL IS TO BELIEVE WE CAN HAVE FULL RELATIONSHIPS WITH OTHERS, WITHOUT INVOKING THE FULLNESS OF CHRIST IN OUR LIVES.

"Pastor Anthony, this book is incredible! It's so crazy to finally understand how men yearn for respect and women yearn for love. Who knew?!" I proclaimed.

During our third marriage counseling session, Kaleb and I sat down telling our pastor all about the great things we learned in a book called *Love and Respect* by Emerson Eggerichs. We excitedly shared the secrets to loving well and having a happy, healthy marriage.

But our pastor met each new concept we shared with, "That's true and good, but you need Jesus."

"Why does he keep saying that?" I thought. "I mean, I know we need Jesus. Duh."

But it's really clear what he meant now. No matter how much revelation or knowledge we have about relationships and how to make them work, it's the brokenness in each of us that desperately needs the perfect wholeness of Jesus.

If two broken people are going to join forces in any capacity, then it would be wise for each one to be totally reconciled to Jesus Christ and intimately acquainted with His perfect love. This love is the only force that truly changes a man or woman, giving us the ability to build something sound and sturdy with our broken bricks.

When it's just us and Jesus, it seems way easier to build a relationship with Him that's healthy and strong. I mean, He's perfect and we aren't, so at least one person in the equation has it all together.

But in friendship, in marriage, and in family, you are dealing with two totally imperfect, broken people. Those two people join together in some capacity and attempt to create something whole, something unified. But how?

That's where the tension builds. That's where the stakes rise. Our own downfall is to believe we can bring wholeness and fullness in our earthly relationships without receiving the holy overflow of water straight from our heavenly Source.

Fill Your Cup

If any specific relationships or people came to mind while reading this, take that as your prompt to assess your role with those individuals. Consider and write down how you can fill the other person's cup rather than drain it today.

As you seek to rebuild or reinforce your healthy relationships, meditate on the truth of Colossians 1:17: "...in Christ all things hold together." Knowing He holds you and your loved one, you can fight for your relationships from a place of inner security and peace.

_____

_____

_____

_____

_____

_____

"For we are God's handiwork, created in Christ Jesus to do good works, which God prepared in advance for us to do."

Ephesians 2:10, NIV

DAY 16: WHEN FORGETTING OUR IDENTITY DRAINS OUR CUP

EACH YES WE GIVE GOD ILLUMINATES THE NEXT STEP TO OUR DESTINY.

"Alexis, I would like you to meet my friend, Frank!" Mr. Chris smiled.

As this tall, weathered man walked up, his furrowed brow and imposing nose made me think he wasn't happy to meet me. But his baseball cap, baseball shirt, tennis shoes, and business cards made me think, "This guy must really like baseball."

"Frank here has an incredible story, and I thought he might be a good fit for your Five Lives speakers series," Mr. Chris said.

Five Lives is a platform my mom and I host where we have different guest speakers come share their life story with a live audience.

"Yeah," Frank grunted.

His callous attitude made me like him even more. So with a beaming smile I asked, "Well, what's your story?"

"…And on her death bed, my wife looked at me and said, 'Frank, you love baseball. But you just like God.' And I told her, 'I know. But I don't know how to love Him.' She said, 'Just ask Him to put love in your heart.' So that's exactly what I did. I've never been the same man since."

Talk about judging a book by its cover. I had no idea that behind this man was a deep loss and an incredible sense of purpose. You see, on most days now, you can find Frank walking up to people in the parking lot or grocery store aisles asking them if they really like their jobs.

"You ask them if they like their jobs?" I asked. "Yup!" he said. "I hand 'em this card right here and I tell 'em I'm an expert at helping people find what they were born to do."

He handed me the card. It was a simple prayer, asking Jesus to come into my heart.

"If I can connect people to their Creator, I can connect them to what He put them on Earth to do!" Mr. Frank explained.

———

Some seasons in life bring more questions about purpose than others. Questions like, "God what do you want me to do after college?!" or "God, am I just supposed to _____ forever?" can bring out more stress than peace because we expect God to reveal our entire story in just one moment, instead of letting Him unravel our story one day at a time. That's why connecting with our Creator in every season is so crucial.

Our identity isn't wrapped up in what we do or what skills we have, it's rooted in being God's chosen, dearly loved child. From that place of security, we are more inclined to give Him our "yes" as soon as He asks something of us. So when we look back at our lives, we will see that these micro-moments of obedience were the tiny lamps that lit the way to our destiny.

In the warm glow of His presence, our anxious questions about purpose and jobs and callings melt into a peaceful, humble surrender.

Fill Your Cup

Do you know what God put you on this Earth to do? Whether that answer is a resounding yes or a frustrated "I don't know," lean into the Holy Spirit in these next few moments. Ask Him what He has for you to do today.

Remember, Christ's burden is light. So, let's take off the pressure and lessen the burden by just focusing on today. Write out what He's speaking to you, who He's highlighting to you.

"But when you ask, you must believe and not doubt, because the one who doubts is like a wave of the sea, blown and tossed by the wind. That person should not expect to receive anything from the Lord. Such a person is double-minded and unstable in all they do."

James: 1:6-8, NIV

DAY 17: WHEN DOUBT IN GOD DRAINED MY CUP

FIRST, DOUBT WILL POKE HOLES IN YOUR CUP. THEN THE SHAME OF DOUBTING WILL SUCK THE LIVING WATER RIGHT OUT OF YOU. BE ON YOUR GUARD.

Tonight while watching a nature documentary, my hands excitedly hit Kaleb's chest as I said, "Can you believe this?! How did God come up with this stuff?! Look at that crab!"

Imaginations of Heaven ran through my mind, wondering what it would be like with a God as creative and unpredictably cool as Him. Then, like a rock hitting my windshield on the interstate: "What if you die and realize there is no heaven and no God?" I thought.

As my thoughts raced to repair the crack, I told myself to lean into my past experience, to remember all God has done for me—but it wasn't enough. Doubt challenged me again, seeking to drain my cup: "What if all of that just happened as a result of life working itself out and time healing you?"

Next, it wasn't a rock that hit my windshield. It was a boulder. "How could you even have allowed such a thought into your mind? Aren't you a Christian?" Shame scolded.

"But have you ever thought of this?" the Holy Spirit offered. "Have you ever thought about the verse in James 1:6-8, that says, 'a person who doubts should not expect to receive anything from the Lord because they're unstable in everything they do?' Think about that and think about this: most likely, you are on the verge of seeing and receiving something GREAT from the Lord. And the devil knows it. And he doesn't want you to receive any good thing from God. So he's tempting you to doubt."

——

Friend, the devil cannot stop God from pouring out His blessings on your life. The devil can merely tempt you to drill those holes in your glass, making doubt your god instead of Jesus, causing emptiness instead of fullness.

If you're struggling with doubt, channel it honestly like the man in Mark 9:24 by crying out, "Lord I believe, help my unbelief."

When we do that, we bring ourselves under the shelter of our loving Father, and we position our hearts to receive and to see the great things God is pouring out on our lives.

Fill Your Cup

Face your accuser in this moment and flush out your doubts. Write them down and pray over these matters of the heart, asking Holy Spirit to help you in your unbelief. He will do it quickly.

_____

_____

_____

_____

_____

_____

_____

_____

"'For I know the plans I have for you,'
declares the LORD, 'plans to
prosper you and not to harm you,
plans to give you hope and a future.'"

Jeremiah 29:11, NIV

DAY 18: WHEN "WHAT IF" DRAINED MY CUP

WHAT IF I TOLD YOU, YOU COULD KEEP YOUR GLASS FROM LEAKING WATER?

Last night as I was lying in bed next to Kaleb, I slowly brought myself to the land of "what ifs." "What am I going to do if Kaleb dies?" What if Kaleb gets really sick?" "What if we end up having another world war and he gets drafted?"

After a few minutes, I jolted my mind and despairingly asked, "Lord, why do I think like this?" Instantly I heard something like this from the Holy Spirit:

"You live in fear instead of faith. You live as though thinking and accepting these potential tragedies will somehow prepare you for when they come. All the while, you're digging trenches in your thought life of dreadful expectations about your future—even though the Bible says God gives you a future and a hope."

——

The truth is, Jesus is the only one who can prepare your heart for what's to come in your life. His role is to defend and protect you from tragedy or in the midst of tragedy. He's the only one who truly knows what's to come, and He's pre-determined to take care of you by commanding His angels to guard you. Be free and rest in the blessed assurance of His love, protection and attention.

Fill Your Cup

Have you ever led yourself to the land of "What Ifs"? Chances are, if you have, it didn't leave you feeling excited and hopeful about your future.

For whatever reason, it's just easier to assume the worst when we start thinking about our lives. It creates a low-risk environment for us, so that if we don't get everything we've hoped for, we're not ashamed or embarrassed or disappointed.

But, Psalm 25:3 says "No one who hopes in you will ever be put to shame" and Psalm 37:4 says "Delight yourself in the Lord, and he will give you the desires of your heart."

So in these next few lines, jot down some of those negative "what ifs" you're battling today. Then, jot down how God's promises tell a better story about your future. Let God breathe hope-filled expectation in you again as you meditate on Jeremiah 29:11, Psalm 25:3 and Psalm 37:4.

_____

_____

_____

_____

_____

_____

_____

_____

"The heart of her husband trusts in her...believes in her securely so that he has no lack...She comforts and encourages and does him only good as long as there is life within her."

Proverbs 31:11-12, AMP

DAY 19: WHEN BELIEVING I WAS A BAD WIFE DRAINED MY CUP

WHEN WE AGREE WITH ANXIOUS THOUGHTS, THE FULLNESS CHRIST PAID FOR SEEPS OUT OF OUR CUPS AND WE LIVE ANOTHER DAY HALF EMPTY.

My eyes were shut but my mind kept chiding me to stay awake, to listen to the endless anxieties about what a terrible new wife I am. "I'm going to end up failing Kaleb. I'm going to end up causing him pain. I'm going to end up being a bad wife."

In a case of self-sabotage, I let the fullness of God leak right on out of me because I was drilling these holes in the bottom of my glass of life—holes of anxiety and condemnation.

As I sunk under the shame of things that haven't even happened, the Holy Spirit raced to my side, "Find a verse for this."

"I think Proverbs 31 says something about being a good wife," I thought. So at midnight, while my sweet husband was fast asleep, I pulled out my Bible.

There it was in Proverbs 31:12, "She comforts and encourages and does him only good as long as there is life within her."

I just kept repeating that line under my breath. I spoke it until my monsoon-sized anxiety dried up into puddle. Those words were just what I needed to hear so I could fill my draining cup again.

The message God had for me that night was the same one He's been weaving gently into my soul for years: I am full.

——

When I play back the tape of that anxious night, something becomes very clear: the Enemy of my soul is slick. When he plants a lie in our minds, he does it in the first person. See, anxiety didn't say, "Alexis is a terrible wife." No, It said, "I am a terrible wife."

Do you see how that carries so much more shame? That first person narrative of negativity cuts our legs out from under us, crippling us in our journeys.

We've all been there—self-sabotaging, sinking under our own criticism and anxiety. But the Lord has a better way. His way leads us in green pastures, guides us beside quiet waters. His way restores our soul (Psalm 23).

And if we want to step into that way of life, we must train our minds to recognize a crippling thought as soon as it attempts to steal our peace from us.

Fill Your Cup

Take these next few lines to remind yourself and the enemy what you are and what you are not. In my personal example I wrote, "I am full. I am NOT a bad wife. I am NOT a failure. I am NOT going to cause my marriage's demise. I WILL do him good as long as there is life in me."

Your turn! What are some thoughts or beliefs keeping your glass from filling up today? Write out the truth about yourself using scripture to reinforce God's view of you.

_____
_____
_____
_____
_____
_____
_____
_____

"When you were dead in your sins and in the uncircumcision of your flesh, God made you alive with Christ, He forgave us all our sins."

Colossians 2:13, NIV

DAY 20: WHEN FEAR OF BEING A FAILURE DRAINED MY CUP

WHEN WE WERE SUPREMELY OFFENSIVE, CHRIST WAS LAVISHLY GENEROUS TOWARD US IN LOVE. IT'S ON THE BASIS OF HIS EXTRAVAGANT LOVE THAT WE MUST FULLY REST OUR IDENTITY.

For months I struggled to take the leap, to venture into the great unknown of entrepreneurship. But why all this struggle when I knew it was my destiny? I interrogated myself until I could name the root of my hesitation.

The root this time was fear (it almost always is). But fear of what? Why am I so afraid to just make a change? Why am I hesitating to just jump off the cliff and go after what I know in my heart I deeply want?

In truth, I was having an identity crisis. I've found so much affirmation in being good at my job, in successfully accomplishing each little item on my to-do list, in managing a low stakes, low reward career.

"But will I be able to handle going out on my own? Will I feel lost and confused when I'm not being told what to do? What about my to-do lists and my team of people who can help me when the going gets rough? What if I hate myself for making the decision? What if I fail?"

Then, like clockwork, that still small voice of the Holy Spirit presented another perspective. He reminded me that whether I stay in this job or create a new career path, my identity would remain unchanged. I would still be totally and completely loved by Jesus, so I didn't need to worry about being labeled a failure.

———

Unlike the world, Jesus doesn't define us by our skillset or accomplishments —none of that propels Him toward us. So if He approves of us fully, what do we have to be afraid of?

On the days you feel shaky, on the days the waves are more prominent, when the tide starts to pull you away, you can anchor yourself to the rock, to the one who has makes you full.

When you're out in life's proverbial sea, the wind of His love will propel you and the comfort of His presence will encourage you.

Fill Your Cup

We can all relate to attaching our identity to something temporary. Whether it's our talent or our career or the familial role we play, there is always the temptation to trust those other sources for affirmation. But this is not the higher way.

When we live fully in Jesus and associate our identity with His unmerited love and acceptance, then we can face any loss or change that comes because we're anchored to the unchangeable God.

Write down some things that you may be tying your identity to. Chances are, most of those identifiers are awesome blessings, so thank God for them! But also ask Him to deepen your understanding of the truth that He alone is your source of fullness and value.

_____

_____

_____

_____

_____

_____

_____

_____

"Finally, brothers and sisters, whatever is true, whatever is noble, whatever is right, whatever is pure, whatever is lovely, whatever is admirable—if anything is excellent or praiseworthy—think about such things."

Philippians 4:8, NIV

DAY 21: WHEN JUDGING MY HUSBAND DRAINED MY CUP

IF COMPARISON STEALS OUR JOY, CRITICISM STEALS OUR DELIGHT—
NOT ONLY IN OURSELVES, BUT IN OTHERS.

"I would like to make a toast to Kaleb and Alexis," my father-in-law beamed. "You know, ever since Kaleb was a little kid, he was just so fun and so interesting to get to watch grow up. He was always just a joy and a delight to raise, and he's still a joy and a delight to this day."

From that night on, Kaleb's contact name was "Kaleb, a joy and a delight" in my brother-in-law's phone. It's a joke between us because at Kaleb's sister's wedding, their dad was sharing embarrassing stories of her—but Kaleb, he got the "joy and delight" treatment.

Now as his wife of two years, I can attest to the incredible, wonderful, fun, honest man he is. But sometimes, I catch myself being critical.

Yesterday, we got up to go serve food to some inner-city families. As my eyes peered over to him getting dressed, I immediately thought, "Now why is he wearing his work clothes to go volunteer? Why doesn't he wear something cute like a pocket tee and the new pants I bought him?"

This is a good time to tell you that once you get married or have any semblance of a deep relationship with someone, your half-empty attitude will affect the atmosphere of your love.

Annoyance started to well up inside of me as I was just about to ask, "Why are you wearing your construction clothes to volunteer?"

But then I heard that inner voice of the Holy Spirit raising the bar for me: "Kaleb is full." There it was: a call not to drain my husband's cup, a call to keep my cup from draining the delight I truly have in him.

In my mind I repeated this truth: "Kaleb is full and he lacks nothing because he is hidden in the fullness of God in Christ."

The urge to criticize and question his apparel fled, and I was so glad. Speaking that one truth over my husband saved us from a messy morning of needless bickering and hurt feelings.

We both served that morning with smiles on our faces, with genuine joy and our night ended with a dance party in our kitchen while cooking Greek food.

———

When we call out the truth of God in the ones we love, our perspective shifts. We start seeing things from our Father's looking glass, instead of our broken one.

Fill Your Cup

Take a minute right now and ask the Holy Spirit to shift your perspective about those around you and about yourself. Wait on Him and let Him show you your life through His lenses.

Then, write out those noble, pure, lovely and admirable thoughts—assign them to your life and to your people.

_____

_____

_____

_____

_____

_____

_____

"Do not let any unwholesome talk come out of your mouths, but only what is helpful for building others up according to their needs, that it may benefit those who listen."

Ephesians 4:29, NIV

DAY 22: WHEN PERFECTIONISM DRAINED MY HUSBAND'S CUP

WHEN WE MEASURE OUR LIVES AGAINST WORLDLY PERFECTION, OUR GLASS WILL ALWAYS FEEL HALF EMPTY.

The other night, Kaleb and I were getting ready for bed while discussing tomorrow's plans. He briefed me on the jobs for the week and his schedule for his team.

Listening to him, I was so impressed with how he manages all of those employees, how he coordinates so many jobs and clients. "Kaleb, you're a really good business owner" I said. "I'm not that good. I drop the ball sometimes, I overbook myself..." he answered.

"Being good doesn't mean you're perfect. You do a really good job and give it your all, and that's what makes you a great business owner," I replied.

"Yeah I guess you're right," he said.

———

How many times a day have we counted ourselves as failures because we weren't perfect? When perfection is the goal, we tend to over-complicate and over-analyze—and that can be paralyzing because the truth is there will always be room for improvement.

When our identity is tied to perfectionism, we often hesitate to pursue our God-given dreams, to test out our new business idea, or to show up to that social event. Fear of messing up stops us before we even give ourselves the chance to try!

Of course working toward excellence is good and important—but unless we build our identity on the solid foundation of Christ, everything we do will eventually crack beneath the pressure of trying to be perfect.

When we remind ourselves that we live and operate in the overflow of Jesus, we can stop striving for perfection and we can take our life's work in strides. As we reinforce that we are full and lack nothing, we can accept our failures and mistakes with grace for ourselves.

I know when it came to writing this book, I put it off for FOUR years because life happened and I felt crippled by the thought of having to make this book totally perfect before I could share it with the world. But finally I realized that the vapor of perfection was just causing me to procrastinate. So before you end up four years in the future without having accomplished your life's work, let's put pen to paper.

Fill Your Cup

What dreams or goals have you been putting off because you're waiting around for perfect conditions before you set sail? Write them down.

Then write some practical steps you can take to get started. Remember, it's not about perfection it's just about starting!

Here's a little example: When I decided to get this book out, I committed myself to writing one chapter a day for thirty days in April. It was a small step and taking it day by day helped me to stay committed to my goal!

Your turn.

_____

_____

_____

_____

_____

_____

_____

"Not that we dare to classify or compare ourselves with some of those who are commending themselves. But when they measure themselves by one another and compare themselves with one another, they are without understanding."

2 Corinthians 10:12, ESV

DAY 23: WHEN COMPARISON DRAINED MY CUP

WHEN WE BELIEVE WE'RE FULL, WE CAN QUIT LIVING IN OUR OWN
MENTAL CHESS GAME WONDERING WHO'S GOING TO MAKE THE NEXT
POWER MOVE.

Our family is pretty big. From brothers and sisters to step-siblings and in-laws, we have a lot of loved ones. But as we get older and grow our immediate families, making time to connect gets harder. So last year, we instituted Family Friday. Once a month, Kaleb's side of the family gets together for a game night with food and lots of quality time.

We have so many dynamics in the room on those nights and it's so much fun. Each couple has their habits, their love languages, their pet peeves—and it's really reassuring to know that Kaleb and I aren't the only two who are constantly working through our own differences and learning curves of marriage.

But on this particular Friday, my cuddly, bubbly night was almost shipwrecked by this one thought (try to contain your laughter): "My sister-in-law and my step-brother's girlfriend have blonde hair, blue eyes; they're stunning. But I look nothing like them. Does that mean I don't fit in with this family?"

I quickly began scanning the room for anyone else who looked like I do, desperately searching for some consolation that I really do belong here. Thankfully, I was quick enough to notice that lie and I immediately retorted, "I am full. I lack nothing. No one is better than anyone or fits in more than anyone because of hair color or appearance."

I wish this was all a joke because it sounds so pathetic. But there are two hilarious truths that my self-conscious anxiety left out of the picture: First, I have tried the whole blonde highlights thing, and it was honestly a terrible look for me. I do not desire to be blonde. Second, my other sister-in-law who wasn't even there that night looks nothing like my other sister-in-law; in fact, she is a completely different race than we are, and she fits in beautifully!

If I had continued down the path of that lie, my whole night would have suffered. I would have started to back out of conversations and back into my own self-absorption, projecting my assumptions of their judgement onto myself. How sad! I would have missed the opportunity to ask with deep sincerity: "How are you doing, sis? What's going on in your life? How can I be encouraging you?" This is the connection we all need.

———

When we enter a room with the mindset that we are full, we get to enjoy life and pursue healthy relationships because we aren't trying to protect ourselves from judgement or criticism. We can quit living in our own mental chess game, wondering who's going to make the next power move.

If we're busy lifting people up and pouring out kindness, we won't have time to pull out our defense mechanisms of jealousy or comparison. Life and relationships are so much sweeter this way.

Fill Your Cup

Most of the time, the thoughts that rob us of joy are thoughts about ourselves. We become so preoccupied with how we're perceived that we become blind to those in need right in front of us. Second Corinthians 10:12 instructs us not to compare ourselves with one another. This is because Christ should be our measuring stick, the one against whom we view ourselves and others. When we use other flawed humans as the ones we compare ourselves against, we will always miss the mark of who God calls us to be.

Scripture tells us Jesus is meek and humble of heart (Matt 11:29), He is full of grace and truth (John 1:14), He is an overcomer (John 16:33). He is patient and long-suffering (Matt 17:17). This is our calling. Write down these attributes of Christ and assign them to yourself (i.e. I am meek and humble; I am long-suffering; I am an overcomer). Declare these characteristics over yourself and live today with Christ as your goal and focus.

"The Lord is close to the brokenhearted and saves those who are crushed in spirit."

Psalm 34:18, NIV

DAY 24: WHEN FATHER'S DAY DRAINED MY CUP

THERE IS NO SAFER PLACE FOR YOU TO ACCESS YOUR PAIN AND
GRAPPLE WITH YOUR GRIEF THAN IN THE PRESENCE OF THE ALL-
SUFFICIENT COMFORTER.

It was Father's Day 2019. The sermon was about, you guessed it, fathers.

"I can do this. I'm good. I'm fine. I had a great dad when he was here," I
thought to myself as the preacher kept sharing.

The sermon was beautiful. My pastor shared the privileges of and purpose of
fatherhood. At about 15 minutes in, he directed his attention to the dads in
the room and emphasized just how much children need their fathers—need
them to lead, need them to engage, and need their time.

My tear ducts rattled. "But what about my need? I need my dad and I can't
have him. Why can't I have him?" I thought.

The floodgates burst, my glass of fullness seeped rapidly. I scrambled for my
pen and journal. Line after line like lightning, "The Lord is my all-sufficient
Father, The Lord is my all-sufficient Father, The Lord is my all-sufficient
Father."

As the free-fall of deep loss drained me, the reassurance of my all-sufficient
Father filled me. I can't even tell you where those words came from; I can
only attribute it to the Holy Spirit rising up in me to comfort me.

With each new line, that phrase pacified my pain. Holy Spirit swooped in
with words I couldn't gather on my own and swiftly rose to reassure His
daughter who deeply misses her earthly father.

———

Sometimes, you have no choice but to ride the wave of pain, and that may
mean bawling crying outside of church or shutting down in the midst of a

social outing. But the internal battle is only lost when we keep our eyes on our pain instead of lifting them up to our all-caring, all-knowing Father.

Fill Your Cup

Have you experienced a deep loss or pain that finds its way into your everyday normal? Do you find that specific holidays make the hurt more prominent? Do you work effortlessly to hold it all together and brace yourself for the worst?

It may not be possible to do on command, but I offer you a moment to breathe deep and tap into the hurts you've carried and managed for so long. Sometimes it takes intentional moments of breathing to realize it's been a long time since you've let yourself come up for air.

Allow yourself to feel, knowing you are safe and held in the arms of your kind, comforting Father. Write down Psalm 34:18 and keep your heart open to receive anything else the Holy Spirit may gently weave into your spirit. Remember, you don't need to be afraid of confronting your past hurts because Christ is close to the brokenhearted.

_____

_____

_____

_____

_____

_____

_____

_____

"The thief comes only to steal kill and destroy, I have come that they may have life, and have it to the full."

John 10:10, NIV

DAY 25: WHEN NOT EXPECTING ANYTHING FROM GOD DRAINED MY CUP

JUST PAST THE MIRACLE OF OUR UNDESERVED SALVATION IS YET ANOTHER GIFT WE HAVEN'T EARNED—A LIFE THAT IS FULL AND ABUNDANT.

On a chilly, sunny afternoon in one of New Orleans' most dangerous neighborhoods, I heard these words in my spirit: "I'm not going to restore you back to the place you were before you experienced the trauma of losing your dad. I am going to restore you far beyond that."

It caught me by complete surprise. It had been four years since my dad passed away and it's been a while since I've asked God to heal me from that trauma. I figured I was as healed as I would ever be.

Just a few months later, our country entered into a nationwide shutdown from the global pandemic of COVID-19. In those months of March and April, I experienced a reawakening of sorts in my spirit.

My work hours went from 40 hours a week to 12 and the majority of my days were free of responsibility. So, I made a pact with myself to write 30 chapters in 30 days, and here we are with the finished product of this devotional.

Those two months felt like returning home. Suddenly, I found myself with ample time to pray, extensive time to write, and the freedom to be alone in the house with just me and God—totally uninterrupted by any other demands of life.

The best way I can describe this time is like dipping into a refreshing spring, revitalizing and reinvigorating parts of me that had fallen asleep in the wake of losing my sweet dad.

You see, after my dad died, a lot of incredible things happened. I got a wonderful job, I married my amazing husband, we bought a ratty, fixer upper house, and we were featured on an international publication for all of our hard work!

Yet while those things filled my cup, and while each day brought meaning and joy and healing to my world, Jesus was still saying, "I have abundantly more."

Those months of social distancing and quiet time and extended room for writing and pursuing my gifts with God—they stirred something up in me. They brought me even further into the "more" that God has. During what could have been a paralyzing, boring, or depressing time in life, God stepped in and healed me even more. You see, April 26th was the day my dad passed away, and this year, I was blissfully unaware that it was even April, the month that for so long brought me dread and sadness.

He's healed me and filled me up to yet another level beyond what I ever even thought possible for myself.

———

Is there any area of your life you've stopped expecting God to move? Any part of you that's sat dormant for too long? Maybe you're grappling with loneliness. Maybe you're desperate for new friends. Maybe you've grown complacent in your walk with God. Maybe you haven't written or painted in a long time. Maybe you've stopped expecting God to do increasingly and abundantly more. Sometimes, it can feel like life is happening for everyone else except you.

Know that Jesus will surprise you with just how extravagant of a giver He is. Know that He cherishes you; His eyes are on you and they are filled with a love we will never fully comprehend on this side of eternity. Rest in that hard-to-believe truth.

Fill Your Cup

Today, know that you can hope for even more from God, without needing to fear that you'll be disappointed. God has even more filling and healing and lavishing for you, if you will yield your life and heart to him.

Take a few minutes and breathe deeply, asking Holy Spirit to come near, to show you what areas of your life you need to yield to Him. Ask Him to increase your faith and rebuild your trust in His goodness.

Write down what comes to you as you meditate on the truth that Jesus wants to give you a life that is full and abundant (John 10:10).

_____

_____

_____

_____

_____

_____

_____

_____

"Come to me, all you who are weary and burdened, and I will give you rest. Take my yoke upon you and learn from me, for I am gentle and humble in heart, and you will find rest for your souls. For my yoke is easy and my burden is light."

Matthew 11: 28-30, NIV

DAY 26: WHEN WORRYING ABOUT LOVED ONES DRAINED MY CUP

WHEN YOU POUR YOURSELF OUT, YOU'RE GIVING GOD THE ROOM HE NEEDS TO FILL YOU UP.

Today felt strange.

I was restless for hours; I couldn't focus on work; none of my usual tricks helped me get in the zone. At the end of the day, I stopped by my sister-in-law's to see how she and her two little girls were doing. My mother-in-law was there too. I loved our time together. Then I left and went back home to meet my father-in-law to help him with marketing for his business. After that, I got back in the car to go meet Kaleb.

But the whole car ride there, I felt heavy and uncomfortable. My in-laws, my friend, my mom, all of these people I love seeped into my mind. "Are they okay? Are they hurting? Are they lonely?" I worried.

My stomach turned.

As I drove down the oak-tree lined avenue, everything blurred.

"What's wrong with me? Lord why do I feel this way? Maybe I just need to watch that tv show I really like. No, that won't fix it. Maybe I need to turn on something funny. No…" I thought.

As I slowed to a red light, the pulsing bass of the nearest car told me I should play some music: "Oh that'll do it. I just need to play a hymn or an old classic from the 60s. Yeah something upbeat. No. I know that won't help me right now…"

Exhale. Breathe.

"Lord, I feel so sad." There, I said it. "Lord, I'm worried about my people."

Exhale. Breathe.

Name by name, I poured it all out. My worries, my questions, placing the people I love in His hands.

Then, a smile, mixed with tears, mixed with the overwhelming relief of His all-sufficiency.

———

God doesn't ask us to shove our feelings away. He doesn't demand we brush off our pain and put on a brave face. He specifically instructs us to come to him and let him carry our burdens, so that HE can GIVE us rest (Matthew 11:28-30).

Phew that's heavy.

Let that sink in for you right now. He wants you to bring him your worries. He wants you to engage Him in your hurt.

It is the only way we can experience His fullness. We have to pour out our entire selves before Him and let Him fill us back up with Himself.

Fill Your Cup

Pour it out today. Right here on these lines, make your burdens known to God and live out Matthew 11:28-30. Make these blank spaces your altar before your Father and empty yourself. Then, breathe as He deposits more of Himself into you. Rest, knowing it's all in His gentle, capable hands now.

_____
_____
_____
_____
_____
_____

"Whatever you do [whatever your task may be], work from the soul [that is, put in your very best effort], as [something done] for the Lord and not for men, knowing [with all certainty] that it is from the Lord [not from men] that you will receive the inheritance which is your [greatest] reward. It is the Lord Christ whom you [actually] serve."

Colossians 3:18-19, 23-24, AMP

DAY 27: WHEN APATHY FOR MY JOB DRAINED MY CUP

WE BRING THE PASSION TO THE PLACE, THE PLACE DOESN'T BRING THE PASSION TO US. WE ARE THE VESSELS.

"My job doesn't bring me passion," I thought, as I typed in defeat and frustration.

My job was a great job. It allowed me to hone my skills, walk in my strengths, and receive incredible benefits like a 401K and healthcare. Plus, four years ago when I started, it provided a low-stress environment where I could work and make money, while having enough mental margin to recover from losing my dad so suddenly.

But today, these thoughts of dissatisfaction seeped into my conscience and drained my cup.

Podcast after podcast told me all about having a passionate and fulfilling career, but I didn't have that. The internal pressure mounted. "I need to find a better career. What am I even doing here? What am I really passionate about?"

I couldn't even focus on my work anymore. But then, I challenged that half-empty mentality with this thought, "I don't need a job to bring me passion. The passion living in me is what brings passion to the job. I can do any job and still do it with passion because Jesus lives in me."

No more defeatist thoughts, no more feeling half empty. My glass was full again.

———

We have ALL been assigned a task or a job that wasn't ideal. But we can live with passionate purpose on the way to our dream job or in the midst of the necessary, mundane tasks of life. We can start living a passionate, purpose-filled life right where we are! We have life Himself inundating us and He can help us live life with excellence.

So, let's be willing to serve our company or our family in whatever capacity the season requires because that, my friend, is where we will be stretched and matured to take on the next big thing—and more importantly, to look more like Jesus.

Fill Your Cup

So let's hash this out. What tasks or jobs in your life just feel like they're draining you completely? Write them out and then dedicate five or ten minutes to really place those things in the light of gratitude and purpose. Ask the Holy Spirit to help you see Heaven's perspective on the things that just seem so insignificant and annoying. He might show you that there's someone at your job He wants you to share the Gospel with, or He may show you how you can be a better servant to your boss or friends.

Whatever it is, jot it down and embrace Colossians 3:18-19 so you can experience His abundant grace for you to do what you do with excellence and purpose.

"God has placed each part in the body just as he wanted it to be. If all the parts were the same, how could there be a body? As it is, there are many parts. But there is only one body."

1 Corinthians 12:18-20, NIV

DAY 28: WHEN FEELING THREATENED BY OTHER PEOPLE'S SUCCESS DRAINED MY CUP

THERE'S ROOM FOR EVERYONE AT GOD'S TABLE, SO WE CAN CHAMPION EACH OTHER WITH GENUINE EXCITEMENT RATHER THAN CALCULATED COMPETITION.

As I finished up the manuscript for this book, my focus shifted to publishing. "How do I do this? Where? Who do I know that can show me?" I thought.

After a few minutes, I reached out to one of my incredibly talented and newly published friends. She happily told me how she did it all, and then we hung up.

"Did she leave any info out? Is she annoyed that I asked? Mad?" I worried.

The tank-empty light flashed in my soul. My thoughts swirled as my mood went from happy and hopeful to nervous and self-conscious.

"Ok, stop." I demanded, as I grabbed the reigns of my mind. "I am full and God is abundant and it does not matter who else is doing what else. There is room for each one of us to pursue our gifts and to write books and to self-publish. Her knowledge and accomplishments do not lessen my purpose."

Just like that, freedom. Just like that, a step closer to my destiny, an ounce fuller than before.

———

If you're up on the stage of life, nervously calculating everyone else's achievements, wondering if they're judging you for trying or laughing at you for succeeding, breathe real deep with me. Remember, we are all unique and we all hold specific talents and purposes. God formed each one of us and He knits us all together in His family, to be one unified body. He makes room for each one of us on the stage.

Now repeat after me, "My God is an abundant God. I am full because of Him and not because of anything I do or have. He has enough room and resources for all of us. He is never lacking."

Fill Your Cup

Now, let's take the time to get God's perspective on you station in life. Is there a leaky faucet in your subconscious that always wonders if "they" are judging you or bored of you or tired of you? Name those people and those judgements you're afraid they're holding against you.

Then, do what Romans 12:14 says, "Bless and do not curse those who persecute you." Write out the names of people who are your competitors or your enemies (or maybe just your friends) and declare a blessing over them. Speak abundance over them and experience your cup filling up as your heart posture changes from inwardly focused, to outwardly focused.

You will find new strength and excitement as you stop feeling threatened by other people's success and start feeling empowered by the many parts of Christ's body who are joining you in making something beautiful on this earth!

_____

_____

_____

_____

_____

_____

_____

_____

_____

"Dear friends, I urge you, as foreigners and exiles, to abstain from sinful desires, which wage war against your soul."

1 Peter 2:11, NIV

DAY 29: WHEN SOCIAL MEDIA DRAINED MY CUP

SOCIAL MEDIA CAN BE A DEADLY TRAP IF WE MAKE IT A SOURCE OF VALIDATION AND IDENTITY.

"Can you talk?" I texted my friend Risa.

She called five minutes later to hear me bursting in tears, while sitting next to my husband on the couch.

"Is everything okay?" she asked.

"I'm so confused and hurt and I don't know what to do. Everything that people are posting on social media is so overwhelming. I feel judged if I say nothing and judged if I say anything."

"You're not alone, Alexis," she said. "My husband and I have talked to so many people who feel exactly like you do. It's a really hard time right now."

———

Every few years, different topics become centerstage on social media. From sexual assault to human trafficking to social injustice, there are many voices and opinions demanding we either speak up or sit down.

Specifically in the past few months, the escalating online peer pressure brought many people exactly where I was: feeling overwhelmed, judged or confused.

But why? As I sat on my couch in tears and overwhelm, I realized my sin. I had taken my eyes off of Christ, and I had looked to social media for answers, for validation, for security. I was measuring myself against other people's opinions instead of Christ's.

The temptation to turn our eyes from Jesus can have fatal consequences if we don't check ourselves and repent. When we enter into a game of trying to please man versus trying to please Christ, we become slaves to popular opinion and we lose the freedom and discernment we have in Christ. But this doesn't have to be.

In a time when digital debates and online opinions beg us to join in, it's imperative that we guard our souls and ground ourselves in the truth that we are just strangers here. We must keep our heavenly citizenship at the forefront of our mind, so that when we engage in society, we do so from a place of love and fullness.

May our heart posture always be one of submission to Christ, recognition of our fullness in Him, and abundance in our love toward others.

Fill Your Cup

Have you ever taken a minute to let the insignificance of social media sink in? Think about it from an eternal perspective. These digital platforms cannot save us, they can't heal us, they can't transform us into better people. In fact, I think it's possible for social media content to become something that wages war against our souls, as 1 Peter states. Yet, we often bury ourselves under the pressure of digital validation.

Remember, Matthew 12:36 says that on Judgment Day, we will give an account for every empty word we have spoken. I believe this includes the words we type, the photos we post, and the videos we share.

Take a moment to let the gravity of Matthew 12 sink in. Repent for any empty words you've spoken or posted and ask God for discernment to know how you can live as a citizen of Heaven while a foreigner here on Earth. Write out what He's speaking to you.

_____

_____

"Do not be anxious about anything, but in every situation, by prayer and petition, with thanksgiving, present your requests to God."

Philippians 4:6, NIV

DAY 30: WHEN ANXIETY ABOUT THE FUTURE DRAINED MY CUP

AS SEASONS CHANGE, THERE IS STILL ONE CONSTANT WHO REMAINS, AND HE'S WAITING WITH WATER THAT WILL MAKE YOUR CUP OVERFLOW.

Yesterday, Kaleb and I found out we are 99.99% pregnant! But I guess when you take three different pregnancy tests—all positive—that 99.99 becomes 100%!

We were so nervous, so excited.

As we scrambled together to meet my mom for Mother's Day dinner, we tried to hide our excitement so she wouldn't catch on. How do moms always know?

From the time between taking the test and showing up to my mom's house, the anxious lies and fears already drilled holes in my cup.

"People who wait longer to have kids have a happier marriage," one lie seethed. "People are going to treat you differently and not respect you as an entrepreneur because you're pregnant," another lie taunted. "Kaleb and you won't ever have alone time again," another lie said.

"Deep breaths," I whispered to myself. "Lord, what do you have to say about all of this?"

"I am knitting that child together in your womb. My hand is making him. Don't be scared. No life happens apart from my hand," I heard in my spirit.

Then, like a waterfall, scripture after scripture came flooding into my cup, filling my soul to the brim.

For the lie that people who wait longer to have kids have happier marriages: "What I, the Lord, have joined together, let no man separate" (Mark 10:9).

For the lie that people will treat me differently when they find out I am a pregnant woman in business: "Trust in the Lord with all your heart and lean not on your own understanding, submit all your ways to him," (Proverbs 3:3).

For the fear that Kaleb and I will never have alone time again: "Do not be anxious about anything, but in every situation, by prayer and petition, with thanksgiving, present your requests to God," (Philippians 4:6).

With promise after promise, the Lord filled my cup to overflowing.

—-

As roles change, people leave, and babies come, there will be many tempting offers to tie our identity to what we have or what we've lost. Yet the more life I experience, the more certain I am that there are only two certainties in life: God and change.

For that reason, we must resolve to drink from His well of life and choose Him as our source of fullness, identity and validation. The world is too fragile to care for us in all the right ways, but Jesus is all-sufficient.

Fill Your Cup

If you're experiencing unexpected changes or need an extra dose of peace, take a moment to meditate on the verses in this chapter. Breathe deep and exhale with gratitude, giving thanks for what you have, for whose you are, and for the gift of fullness. Then, share your heart, your concerns with your Father.

On these lines, jot down some verses that will shield you against whatever lies or fears you're hearing in your mind today.

_____

"Jesus answered, 'Everyone who drinks this water will be thirsty again, but whoever drinks the water I give them will never thirst. Indeed, the water I give them will become in them a spring of water welling up to eternal life.'"

John 4:13-14, NIV

DAY 31: MY CUP OVERFLOWS

THERE IS NO OTHER GOD WHO WALKS RIGHT THROUGH OUR SOCIAL CONSTRUCTS, RIGHT PAST OUR MORAL FAILURES, AND STRAIGHT INTO OUR HEARTS—ALL SO WE CAN KNOW THE FULLNESS OF LIFE WITH HIM.

"Now he had to go through Samaria. So he came to a town in Samaria called Sychar, near the plot of ground Jacob had given to his son Joseph. Jacob's well was there, and Jesus, tired as he was from the journey, sat down by the well. It was about noon. When a Samaritan woman came to draw water, Jesus said to her, "Will you give me a drink?" (His disciples had gone into the town to buy food.) The Samaritan woman said to him, "You are a Jew and I am a Samaritan woman. How can you ask me for a drink?" (For Jews do not associate with Samaritans.) Jesus answered her, "If you knew the gift of God and who it is that asks you for a drink, you would have asked him and he would have given you living water."

"Sir," the woman said, "you have nothing to draw with and the well is deep. Where can you get this living water? Are you greater than our father Jacob, who gave us the well and drank from it himself, as did also his sons and his livestock?"

Jesus answered, "Everyone who drinks this water will be thirsty again, but whoever drinks the water I give them will never thirst. Indeed, the water I give them will become in them a spring of water welling up to eternal life."

The woman said to him, "Sir, give me this water so that I won't get thirsty and have to keep coming here to draw water."

He told her, "Go, call your husband and come back."

"I have no husband," she replied. Jesus said to her, "You are right when you say you have no husband. The fact is, you have had five husbands, and the man you now have is not your husband. What you have just said is quite true."

"Sir," the woman said, "I can see that you are a prophet. Our ancestors worshiped on this mountain, but you Jews claim that the place where we must worship is in Jerusalem."

"Woman," Jesus replied, "believe me, a time is coming when you will worship the Father neither on this mountain nor in Jerusalem. You Samaritans worship what you do not know; we worship what we do know, for salvation is from the Jews. Yet a time is coming and has now come when the true worshipers will worship the Father in the Spirit and in truth, for they are the kind of worshipers the Father seeks. God is spirit, and his worshipers must worship in the Spirit and in truth."

The woman said, "I know that Messiah" (called Christ) "is coming. When he comes, he will explain everything to us." Then Jesus declared, "I, the one speaking to you—I am he" (John 4:4-26, NIV).

———

Have you ever found yourself in an ordinary moment, just like this woman, thirsting for something more? Grappling with a sensation of emptiness? Maybe just for a second, maybe for a season. Have you ever traveled from one well to another, looking for someone or something to quench your thirst, but finding nothing satisfies you? I have.

I spent so many years lending my heart out to people, to causes, to passions, only to find myself just as empty as before. But, at the intersection of my dire thirst and my unshakeable sins, Jesus met me. Without warning, the King of Kings stepped into my world, walked right past my walls and sat with me. He told me, "You can keep drinking this water, the water you've been used to your entire life. But, you will become thirsty again. Or you can drink my water. You can experience eternal life welling up in you until it overflows."

Fill Your Cup

What greater story for us to end with than this? The story of a woman who spent a lifetime filling her own cup at the well, but finding her glass perpetually half empty—until Jesus met her. He walked right in the middle of the life she was living, the sin she was carrying, the emptiness she was bearing. Can you feel the heaviness of this moment?

Maybe her story is all too real to you. Maybe you find yourself still thirsting, still questioning, still hurting. Jesus knows. He watches you every day as you draw from your well. His caring eye follows you to even the darkest places.

Today, may you take Him up on His invitation to eternal life. May you look up from your well and invite Him to fill you. If you're ready to give your whole self to God, all you have to do is tell Him. Say, "God, I need help. I need you to show me you're real. I want to live for you, to live a life that's full and free from the sins I keep falling into. I'm turning from my own way and I am coming to you. Make me clean, fill me with your Holy Spirit, and lead me into an eternal life with you."

Take these next few lines and just talk to Him. Feel free to write out your heart's cry to Him, confess your sins to Him, renew your commitment to Him. Then, enjoy the full, overflowing life welling up inside of you.

_____

_____

_____

_____

_____

_____

_____

_____

_____

CLOSING THOUGHTS

Well, we made it to the end! Wow. Thank you, thank you, thank you! I am so grateful for the gift of your time during these 31 days.

While these stories were snippets of my life and my attempt at living fully, I hope the prompts sparked you to apprehend fullness yourself. I hope my broken efforts brought a new perspective on wholeness and its reality even in the most unlikely of seasons.

As you venture onward and put this book on the shelf, I hope you always remember that you are called by God, you lack nothing, and you are the most powerful force on Earth when you walk in the fullness of your true identity.

Who knows, the next time we hear from each other might be on the other side, when we're basking in the magnitude of Christ's love and sharing glory stories of the full lives we lived.

With love,

Alexis Klein

THE END